THE SAGA OF A CANADIAN TYPHOON FIGHTER PILOT

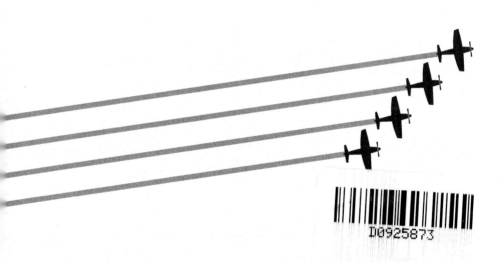

Jack Henry Hilton C.D.

Flight Lieutenant, RCAF (Ret.)

Medal of Friendship Belgium

Legion of Honour France

The Saga of a Canadian Typhoon Fighter Pilot

Tellwell Talent

www.tellwell.ca

ISBN
Paperback: 978-1-987985-73-3
eBook: 978-1-987985-74-0

I dedicate this book to my beloved wife, Ethel Hilton, who, for 71 years has been by my side supporting me in all of my endeavors. None of my life's work would have been possible without this incredible woman. Marrying her was the best decision of my life.

CONTENTS

THE SAGA OF A CANADIAN TYPHOON FIGHTER PILOT

PREFACE

AFTER SPENDING YEARS AS A HAWKER TYPHOON FIGHTER PILOT in both the Canadian and British Air Force during World War II, I have learned that our stories have gone untold.

My squadron and fellow pilots primarily flew the Hawker Typhoon, which has not been recognized by historians. The glamorous Hurricane and Spitfire aircraft seem to be the focus of War stories, overshadowing Typhoon pilots.

The Typhoon was, in spite of numerous technical flaws, the finest close-support aircraft of the War, able to range far and wide over Northwest Europe, providing effective ground attack. During August of 1944 near Falaise France, the Typhoons unleashed bombs, rockets and cannon fire debilitating close to 100% of the German fighting force and vehicles.

We got shot at going in, shot at going out, shot at while trying to sleep, we flew an airplane many tried to avoid having to fly, we did the best with what we had, and somewhere down the line the historians need to pay attention to this astounding history of air warfare.

The Typhoon was a very difficult plane to fly, the Germans hated us as we did so much interdiction, interfering with their transportation and ground forces and with this document the recognition for this aircraft will be given.

The pilots from the 438th, 439th and 440th Squadron RCAF serving in Europe and the 193rd Squadron in the RAF have never received the recognition that they truly deserved.

My hope is that with the telling of my personal story I can shed some light on the amazing men who didn't get the chance to share their stories.

THE EARLY YEARS

I WAS BORN APRIL 1919, IN TORONTO AT MY GRANDPARENTS' house on Boulton Avenue. My parents, my older brother Bill and I moved to Scarborough where my father started building our house. We lived in a train box car for two or three months, getting our water from a well next door, which required a fire started on it in the wintertime to get it going. Eventually we moved into our own house, where Bill and I shared a room and slept in single beds. We had a mattress for a front door until we got an actual door. My father worked two weeks on and two weeks off for the School Board in Toronto. He was proud as punch with our new house and I don't blame him. He had a big lot, 200 ft long and 50 ft wide and we were right at the end of it.

I went to Birchcliff public school and eventually to Scarborough Collegiate as it was called at the time, I went through grade 12 graduating in '36 or '37. I played on the school football team and, although poorly equipped, we won the championship. We played the whole 60 minutes and we had a one-armed kicker. I also played the position of catcher with the school baseball team. After high school I was recruited by Eddie Shore, manager of the Springfield Indians hockey team to play goalie. The goalie job did not work out so I went off to work in the gold mine.

While in High School I had occasion to rescue a young child who had slipped down the side of a cliff. I was about 16 when I did this, I never learned the name of the kid and the parents never thanked me. They were wringing their hands and wondering what to do, so I took a wire that was hanging off the cliff, walked down the side of the cliff, picked up the little guy, wrapped him in my jacket, walked him around to the stairs, went up the stairs and brought him home. A newspaper reporter who lived down the street from me wrote up a big article, and the principal of the school hauled me up in front of my fellow students and commended me for being a hero. I was totally embarrassed but it did pay off with the girls, they wanted to dance with me at the parties!

After grade 12 I got a job through a friend up at Red Lake Gold Mine so I went up by train to Sioux Lookout, then took a float plane to Red Lake. I was a gofer, more or less, I distributed kitchen rations, and also guarded dynamite with a 22 rifle. I roomed with a big Swede, Ivan and I mean he was big, treating me like a son. He'd go to the bar and take me along where I had orange juice and he'd drink beer. On one occasion, he was so protective that when a drunk bumped into me, he just picked him up by the seat of his pants and his collar and threw him right through the door. When we flew out of the gold mine to Sioux Lookout, Ivan and his friend were so drunk they were on the floor of the airplane and I sat up front with the pilot. When we got to Sioux Lookout we had to wait for the train so they gave me their money, $6,000 each, for safekeeping while they cruised the bars. I put them on the train, put their money into each of their pockets and never saw them again.

I returned to Toronto and enlisted in September, 1939 at the age of 19.

FAMILY HISTORY

MY MOTHER, EVA ELIZABETH HILTON (NEE HUNTER) WAS BORN IN Buffalo, N.Y. where her brother, Bill joined the Rough Riders and rode with Teddy Roosevelt in Cuba. He contracted malaria there so he moved to Toronto while her other brother, Jack, moved to Toronto and then lived in North Bay, Ontario representing Underwood Typewriters. Jack would come to Toronto occasionally and he would take me to the early morning horse races and that was a thrill of a life-time. I think he liked to gamble as we'd watch the horses exercise at 5:00 in the morning, then he'd place bets and then the real treat was him taking me to breakfast. For me that was living high off the hog!

My family were very church-oriented, no liquor in the house, we went to church in the morning on Sunday, I went to Sunday school in the afternoon, and we all attended church at night.

It was quite a culture shock when I went from this protected house-hold to the military where I bunked with 5,000 men and saw more liquor spilled than I'd ever seen in my whole life. Being a non-drinker, I was always welcomed to the party so I could take everyone home afterward.

I never heard my father swear in all the time I lived in the house. He smoked one cigar a week, that was his allowance because we were poor. He would sit out in the yard and smoke his 5 cent cigar as his reward for the whole week's work. He made $30 a week, gave it to my mother, and how she fed two hungry teenagers I will never know. She made her own bread and I used to help stir the dough and boy was it beautiful bread.

My Grandmother on my father's side, whom I never met, had 13 children. Grandfather Joseph Hilton came over from England with the two oldest children, both boys. My Grandfather got a job as a blacksmith. My Grandmother then joined him with their four daughters. Then they had 7 more children, with my Dad being the last child. Oddly enough, only the three boys married and had children. While their ten sisters, although marrying, in some cases several times, never had children.

My Grandmother was a very staunch Protestant and you couldn't read the funnies, shine your shoes or cook on Sundays, you just sat around like a lump. She had died before I was aware of the many things she had accomplished. She was a very stern, tough old lady and she used to get on a soap box in downtown Toronto and preach to the Protestants about how the Catholics had an orphanage and the

Protestants did not; she used to take orphans into her home as well.

She spearheaded a drive through the Lady Verner True Blue Lodge to establish an orphanage for Protestant children. Eventually land was purchased and the orphanage was built in Picton, Ontario, with additional property purchased at Richmond Hill in 1919.

At the same time she baked bread in her home and she sent my two uncles door-to-door with baskets of bread to sell. It developed such volume that she moved into a commercial building and ran a bakery. My father eventually worked for his two older brothers at the Bakery. It became so successful that George Westin Bakeries bought them out as they were the only bakery in Toronto. My two uncles, Zeph and Dave , as the two major shareholders took their money and had a good life, moving to Florida. They owned a great deal of property around downtown Toronto but lost it for non-payment of taxes. My father was the worker so he kept working for George Westin Co. who offered him the Eastern franchise but he declined and went to work for the Board of Education as a maintenance, custodial, jack-of-all-trades employee.

ENLISTMENT — TORONTO, ONTARIO

I ENLISTED IN THE AIR FORCE ON SEPTEMBER, 1939 IN TORONTO, Ontario at the age of 19. I did not enlist because of loyalty to King and Country rather I wanted as much control of my destiny as possible and didn't want to be conscripted to be a master potato peeler somewhere in the military. My call-up date was June, 1940 as Aircraftsman 1st class.

My first posting was to the Manning Depot on the Exhibition Grounds in Toronto in 1940. With 5,000 other men, I shared the accommodations they called the Sheep Pen because it was used by the Toronto Exhibition in the summertime for livestock storage. We were issued odd coloured uniforms, flannel shirts, and various pieces of sundry equipment including button plates for polishing, a Ross rifle, grey wool blankets and heavy wool socks to name a few items.

Our Drill Sergeant was from Quebec and his job was to teach us our left foot from our right. His accent made it difficult but we all got the idea. However teaching us rifle drill was enough to give a Drill instructor a heart attack. We got enough inoculations to put us all in bed for a week to recover. Breakfast was oatmeal slopped on a plate. It was something to see and something to experience.

Entertainment was us marching in our heavy boots and wool uniforms around the grounds of the Toronto Exhibition, in July, for the benefit of American tourists. After six weeks we were included in a volunteer program around the base and learned the very first rule-- never volunteer. While we were waiting for assignment, we drilled and kept busy. I wouldn't volunteer to drive a Cadillac, but I did volunteer to type and ended up at the Fire Brigade which was full of friends and relatives. I did very little but tried to look busy which prepared me for ITS (Initial Training School).

ITS posting was to the Eglington Hunt Club in Toronto. There we were processed into the aircrew routine with Link Trainer training; math, military discipline, rules and regulations. The Link trainer is an airplane cockpit, with a cover over it, putting the student into a night environment to learn instruments. It was an early form of a flight simulator that they use today to train jet pilots. My selection came as a pilot while I had wanted to be an air gunner...I like guns. Evidently my Link Trainer Instructor saw something in my coordination that I hadn't noticed and my instrument flying and coordination were acceptable. Now we were entitled to wear the white flashes on our wedge cap, which told everyone who knew that we were selected as aircrew trainees after graduation.

Very few of us had any flying experience, while mine had consisted of being a passenger in a bush plane flying into Red Lake, Canada for work in a gold mine. This is a remote northern Ontario area full of trees, water and creatures I would rather not have to meet and I was nervous the whole time.

After graduation from ITS in Toronto, there was a bottleneck of aircrew training so some of us were sent to guard crates of aircraft at RCAF Trenton, Ontario. We had rifles and bayonets, but no ammunition to scare the seagulls. Duty was four hours on and four hours off and was boring as heck. For a change we were sent to guard a warehouse on the Toronto waterfront. Wintertime on the Toronto waterfront was far from enjoyable and when we found out we were guarding a warehouse full of mattresses it was even less enjoyable.

ELEMENTARY FLYING SCHOOL — WINDSOR AND BRANTFORD, ONTARIO

NOW COMES THE FUN PART. A POSTING TO ELEMENTARY FLYING School at Windsor, Ontario began our flying training. We were introduced to the Fleet Finch, a biplane with a radial engine, and cockpit front and back where the instructor shouted into a tube which went from his backseat to the trainee in the front and very little was understood. The tube was connected to a tube inside the airplane and the instructor would shout through the speaker at his end into my helmet through this tube. My instructor, Sergeant Eaton trained me mostly by hitting the back of my head if I had goofed. He hit me a lot while I learned. We were expected to solo--fly the plane alone--with eight hours of instruction. With our heavy teddy bear flying suits, parachute and helmet goggles, it was a wonder we fit into the aircraft and there was no heat to spoil us.

Two-seater Fleet Finch

Tube hanging from chest to communicate with back seat

Aircraftsman 1ˢᵗ class Jack Hilton in teddy bear flight suit

After 25 flying hours we were now lean, mean fighting machines--veritable balls of fire. Myself, I soloed in the required eight hours. My solo flight took three circuits for me to get that stupid thing down. I was so mad at the airplane, I was going to get it down even if it killed me. Looking back it is a wonder we weren't all killed! I did a ground loop, but I got it down. It scared the living bejesus out of me when the tail of the plane started grabbing me and turning the entire airplane to another direction ... thus ground loop.

The Fleet Finch was noted for an inverted spin characteristic so everyone was careful not to stall during a loop. The answer to getting out of an inverted spin was found to be by opening the coupe top and this changed the plane's attitude. My instructor, Sergeant Eaton, had bailed out on one of these occasions. We became experts in forced landing procedures and this training helped me in my other service flying.

Then we were promoted to the Service Flying School on to the Service Flying School in Brantford, Ontario to learn to fly the Avro Anson. This is a twin engine aircraft that was an old bomber used by the RAF but was sent to Canada to be used as a trainer. The step from a Fleet Flinch to a twin engine airplane was quite a step. The Anson had an air bottle used for braking and your hands had to be crossed. one hand on the twin throttles and one hand on the brake lever. The pedals controlled the air to the wheels and brakes. We received a total of 50 hours training on the Anson.

Avro Anson port side

Avro Anson cockpit view

Avro Anson starboard side

Once flying, the Anson was forgiving and steady. The landing speed was about 70 mph and the top speed was all of 90-95 mph. Hours on this aircraft allowed me to receive my wings as a qualified pilot in the RCAF. My total flying experience: 125 flying hours. Was I ever the expert!

I felt qualified to fly in combat on a heavy bomber but it was not to be.

Sergeant Pilot Jack Hilton

Sergeant Jack Hilton

Instead I was off to RCAF Trenton for a flying instructor's course. Dodging equipment that was constructing a runway, we landed and took off on the grass. After 325 hours of flying, approximately 6 months, I was a qualified flying instructor. Now that I was trained to teach others how to fly with my vast knowledge and experience, I held the high rank of Sergeant and was as proud as could be. From Airman 1st class to Sergeant in less than 6 months, not bad for a green kid from Scarborough, Ontario.

We were given a list of postings requiring flying instructors. My roommate had trained at SFTS in Macleod, Alberta and in my ignorance I asked him where Macleod was located. As a kid from Scarborough, Ontario was the edge of the world as I knew it. When he informed me that Macleod was in Alberta, I was none the wiser. He did say it was as far West as Training Command operated, and as I was overrun with crying relatives in Toronto and eager to see the world, I put my choice down as Macleod. My family didn't get excited about this choice because they had no idea where Macleod actually was and didn't try to figure it out. I wanted away from my many relatives so this worked for me.

No one in eastern Canada wanted a posting out West. Heaven forbid! Everyone was trying for cities and towns throughout Ontario, close to their Toronto home, which is the center of the universe, so my choice was joyfully accepted by Training Command.

1940 graduation class of flight instructors. Jack Hilton, top row second from right.

FLIGHT INSTRUCTOR – MACLEOD, ALBERTA

WITH BASKETS OF FOOD, LOUD WAILING, HUGS AND KISSES FROM elderly relatives, I arrived at Union Station in Toronto for departure. Of course the station seemed to be full of tearful relatives--all seeming to be mine--to my dismay. An embarrassment for a Sergeant Pilot, I was now a fully trained warrior at the age of 20, girded for battle, with all of this confusion around me. Fortunately in those days the conductor sat near the platform and he smiled as I checked in. His comment "too many relatives, son?" made him my friend immediately. My answer, strictly military, "yes sir, you can see the problem." He said "for you, the train leaves now". What a relief when I climbed on the coach and loosened my tunic. Covered with lipstick and the smell of lilacs, Lifebuoy soap, and the other perfumes ladies used in their later years, I happily sat for the hour before the train left, in total peace.

This was my first ever trip on a train and I learned in no time not to fill the basin full of water when the train is moving, it makes for a wet lap. To eat in a dining car was new. I gave my meal ticket to the waiter and the food was much better than military meals! The sights while we were moving kept me busy and the sight of the rails in the distance out of Winnipeg, Manitoba was a great delight. In those days in took four days and three nights to cover the miles from Toronto to Macleod and in that time I learned how to put my pants on while in a berth, shave with very little water, and have my boots polished by a porter. What a life!

Exciting stops like Indian Head, Regina, and Medicine Hat! Wow! It was a taste of the old Wild West. My eyes were like saucers most of the time although I pretended to be a world traveler. I knew my fellow passengers were amused at my expressions. The porter and waiters were most kind to this lonely Sergeant Pilot heading to the wild and unknown destination of Macleod, Alberta.

At last the conductor called the Macleod next stop. To say my heart was in my mouth was an understatement. I was plain scared. When the train stopped, I stepped down and found the West. Pausing for a moment, the Station Agent Mr. McBride met me at the train and said "what's the matter son...lost?" I turned to him and said "Sir, with these Rockies, blue skies and prairie, I'm home".

Arriving at a new base, down the road from the railway station, I reported to the orderly room for processing and getting settled into the Sergeants' quarters and mess. With a war on, no time was lost in sending me to the Flight Commander. Flight Lieutenant T. Delahaye greeted me with "climb into an Anson for a check ride." We tooled around and I suppose I was accepted because Delahaye said "report tomorrow morning, you have four students to train to fly the Anson." No fooling around when there was a war to be won and pilots were badly needed. For two years I graduated over 200 Australian, New Zealand and Canadian young men up to wing standard.

Macleod runway with many Ansons

Flight Instructor Hilton, center, with four students

After many students had graduated under my instruction, one in particular was assigned to me, a New Zealand student named Paterson. The last name is always used in the military. He was placed in my charge to wash out--leave the aircrew training, it was an awful job to have. Wing Commander Brown told me I was to do that after giving him a check ride. Turns out this student had never been given the chance to learn by his instructor. He was from New Zealand, he was homesick, missed his girl and he had a lousy instructor. I took him out in the Anson and I told him to go. He said go where--he'd never taxied. I told him to do his take-off check, which he did beautifully but he had never taken off, this poor kid! I showed him how to take off and then I purposefully folded my arms and said "take off". We went down that runway like a jackrabbit! he did his circuit and then I told him to land. He said he'd never landed...he landed. My report to the Wing Commander was just that--lousy instructor, capable student, his solution...I had another student given to me-- five in total, four normally. Paterson graduated first in his course and won his wings and a Distinguished Flying Cross (DFC). Later when I was in England, I saw him in London, sitting on a bench opposite the palace. I asked him what he was doing there and he said "well Sarge, I just got the DFC". I asked him what in hell he did right. He said "I brought a Halifax there and back with 7 injured flight mates". I said "good for you" so I guess my training paid off! Instructors did not become friends with students, there was a distinction in rank which kept things on a very professional level but it was very satisfying to see Paterson achieve this high award.

I did socialize with other instructors, occasionally; we would go over to Waterton to town parties. It was interesting because the guy had a two seater so the other two would sit in the trunk and hold the lid up as we toured southern Alberta. Obviously great speed was not a problem and it allowed us to survey the landscape. In those days the Indians still buried their people in trees or on tall scaffolding built for that purpose and we would see these structures as we drove around the prairies.

During this period the town of Macleod threw a big party and that was where I met and married Ethel Jane MacRae who worked as a civilian secretary on the base. We danced together, then I took her to a coffee shop, and dropped her off at home. That was the beginning of a friendship that lasted 70 years. We went to the hardware store and paid $5 for the marriage license and shocked her mother and dad. I had gone home to her house and we had whipped cream and chocolate eclairs before we went to bed! In my household, it was pretty strict and we never ate anything before we went to bed! The wedding was all set up and my brother Bill came down from the Alaska highway and his wife Mildred joined us at our wedding in Stirling. We had Stella, as bridesmaid, a friend of Ethel's. Marrying Ethel was the best decision I have ever made in my entire life. Of course we had to get permission to marry and our honeymoon was a 48 hour pass which we spent in the Palliser Hotel, in Calgary, Alberta. October 23, 1942 was the beginning of 71 years of joy. My rank was now Warrant Officer, 2nd class with pay that was all of $4.00 per day, uniform included. We lived in a boarding house in Macleod when we first got married with one room, $30 a month and shared the bathroom down the hall with two other couples. The refrigerator was a box out on the window ledge and the kitchen was a joke. Fortunately for me, Ethel had a great sense of humor and always appreciated the ridiculous! We lived there about 6 months until we were transferred to Bagotville.

As Flying Instructor I was obligated to handle the flying control at night, which consisted of a kitchen chair at the end of the runway, a green aldis lamp with a battery and a red aldis lamp with a battery. An aldis lamp is a portable spotlight, controlled with a trigger which you used to flash Morse code. While we just used red to go around again, green to land, aldis lamps were used by the Navy to signal Morse code. Our aircraft, on their downward leg, would flash their identification signal for permission to land and I, as a flying instructor, sitting in the kitchen chair would hold up one or the other--red or green to them. It was very successful, except you nearly froze to death sitting out there for all of the night flying hours and, of course in the winter your night flying hours were longer than your summer. Eventually someone got smart and bought a little wagon with an old gunnery cover on it and we sat in that out of the wind and gave our landing signals.

The runway had no approach lights along the edges, just farmer lamps, One night I was flying with Ferguson, we took off and flew out into the country learning different aspects of night flying. Then I told him to come into the circuit, which he did, coming in at 1,000 ft over the end of the runway and he did his turn but I watched him and in his turn he wasn't straight, he drifted off course, so he was busy, wheels down, going through his procedure. When I asked him where he was going he said he was going to land on the runway, right straight ahead of him. I told him he was going to land on the main street of Macleod with all of the telephone poles and streetlights. Your runway is over to the left, barely visible. He was very embarrassed, corrected himself and successfully landed, but it shows you how easy it is to get distracted when flying at night.

FIGHTER AIRCRAFT TRAINING – BAGOTVILLE, QUEBEC

AT THIS TIME, COMMAND DECIDED THAT, AS A TWIN ENGINE pilot, I should go to Bagotville, Quebec to train on the Hurricane aircraft, a single engine fighter. This documents the genius of command and I did not volunteer...having learned that lesson from the very beginning.

February 1943 was the last time at #7 SFDS Macleod as an instructor. I was posted to #10 course, 102 Bagotville, Quebec for fighter training. Our greeting at Bagotville by the Wing Commander Flying who informed us that 50% of our #10 course would not go home due to fatalities. That was a cheerful note. I started the 7th of April, 1943 in Bagotville on the fighter course where we, first of all, flew the Harvard...again. I got practically a whole month of Harvard flying, learning sector recon, low flying, solo, you name it, and then I was checked out.

My first trip in a Hurricane was on the 27th of April, 1943 with a sum total of one hour of sector recon training as they called it, which was looking over the countryside, then back into the Harvard for more instrument flying. Harvards were pretty good because they had dual controls. The rest of the training time was on the Hurricane, low flying, sector flying, aerobatics, tail chasing, flying formation, crossover turns, which was unusual, and attacking other aircraft. Crossover training was formation flying two airplanes, one below the other. The wingman is below and when the top plane wanted to go into a dive, say to the right, you went underneath him and did a crossover turn and came up by his left wing. It was a maneuver designed to maximize your diving ability and minimize collisions. Quite often we did a crossover turn if we were being jumped by German airplanes so the wingman would be on the left side and the #1 man would be turning into the German fighters, allowing for two planes flying into the German fighters.

Hurricane fighter plane front view

Hurricane fighter plane in profile

On the 7th of February, when I was at a height of 25,000 ft my engine blew. As I was coming down to 7,000 ft the plane kicked out a piece into the fuel line. I looked like a sign flyer with all the coolant going out of my engine and coming out the stacks. I had a choice, bailout over a field of pine trees, which wasn't a very attractive option, or find an open field surrounded by high tension wires from the Arvada dam which was my choice. As I crash landed the smoke was still pouring out of my plane, when a priest who had been following my descent in his car, jumped up on my wing and said "my son, my son I'm giving you the last rites of the church". I said "thanks father, I'm not of your faith but I appreciate your kindness". We went back to the parish to wait for the rescue crew and we had a beautiful steak dinner. In wartime that was a great treat and he also had bowls of milk covered with cream. I thought I had died and gone to heaven.

On the 8th, I was flying again. No medical checkup, no nothing, the army took me back to the lodging house where we lived and I was flying the next morning at 8:00 a.m. If you were warm, you fly. If you were in the service and if you went on medical leave more than a few times, they Classified you as LMF – lacking moral fibre. Now they call it battle fatigue, but if you were Classified as LMF you would be reassigned and end up doing some dirty job, a "joe job" is what we called it and nobody wanted that.

Crashed plane front view

Crashed plane engine compartment

BE 473   13-MAY 43

Belly landed plane crash

Doug Douglas, who shared an apartment with Ethel and I, along with his wife and baby had gone home and told my wife that the plane I was flying had crashed with me in it. Then he walked away, leaving Ethel in distress. When she asked about my condition, his remark was that I had been picked up by the army and was fine. Doug was in the flight course for the same training as I was getting, so you would think he'd be a bit more sensitive to the feelings of other family members but that was not to be. He died later in a friendly fire incident.

This training course was three months, and at all times Hurricane aircraft were on readiness to protect the dam at Arvada, Quebec as well as the power grid.

Arvada Dam standby air cover – variety of craft

Arvada Dam air cover force

At the close of my course on May 25th I was transferred to the 118th Fighter Squadron on Annette Island, Alaska, U.S.A. Now there was a kick in the head, I thought I was headed for Europe.

On our way to the west coast, we stopped over in Stirling, Alberta, to drop my wife Ethel off with her parents, Alex and Ida MacRae to await the arrival of our first child.

118TH FIGHTER SQUADRON – ANNETTE ISLAND, ALASKA

I REPORTED TO THE OFFICE OF THE MILITARY AT PRINCE RUPERT, British Columbia and I was booked onto a ship going to Annette Island leaving on June 29th, 1943. When I reported to the dock I found I was going north on a tugboat which left at dusk to eliminate sub attacks.

We arrived in the dark with a very heavy fog, and I don't know how the tugboat captain found the place. An American army sentry was walking up and down with a rifle and a jeep took me to my squadron to meet Pete Wilson, Flight Commander of 118th squadron, RCAF Annette Island, Alaska. This was my introduction into the war in the Pacific. Annette Island was a USAF base across from Ketchican and had an RCAF squadron of P40 fighters and a military hospital. The Squadron Leader was Frank Grant who had served previously in Europe.

Once we arrived in Alaska we had no communication with anyone. There were no phones to call out and we were on radio silence anyway.

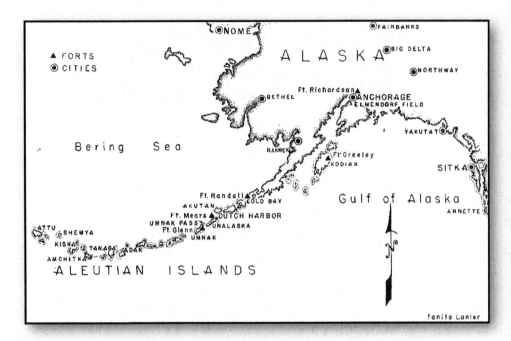

Map of area

We had a gravel runway and metal Nissan huts for accommodations, all connected by duckboards over the bog. Washing our clothes consisted of pressing down on the bog for water to surface and dipping our dainties. To fly the P40 we were given a trip on the Harvard aircraft while flying from the back seat to simulate the attitude of the P40. Then we were briefed on the Kitty Hawk or P40 as the Americans referred to it and sent on our merry way. Fortunately for me, I

Jack Hilton, Flying Officer, RCAF

had more flying experience than some so I had very little difficulty handling the aircraft.

I was promoted to Flying Officer, receiving flight pay of $4 per day and I got 16 trips in the P40 doing patrols over the Pacific. One of our squadron had shot down one Japanese float plane, but none of the rest of us had any combat experience. We flew with a dingy under the seat as our rescue vehicle as air-sea rescue was non-existent, with chances of survival minimal, just "good luck". We looked for carriers but they never did appear, as our flight range was constrained by volume and they never ventured close enough.

Fog was our enemy and very unpredictable so that with our limited radio range we kept a close eye on the weather. One of my sorties consisted of me looking for Japanese aircraft carriers and finding myself on the return home barely getting to the runway ahead of the fog. It was so dense that a tractor or mule was sent to tow me into the dispersal area, which is a place designated for storing the aircraft, supplies, and if pilots were on alert, they would be in the dispersal area in order to quickly take off.

118th, Flight Squadron consisted of 28 pilots, all in various stages of experience with most of the pilots not logging more than 500 hours. I was the only one with over 2500 flying hours due to my instructor experience. This helped to keep me alive, although fate always enters into the equation.

We maintained patrols over the Pacific, but to be honest this seemed to be lacking in any planning or operational sense between the Squadron and any headquarters. There was very little sharing of any information from the top of the Squadron down to us "grunts". It was strange to me why we did not have air-to-ground firing of our aircraft, diverse bombing exercises and a set schedule or rotation of air patrols. Any enemy air activity would have caught us with our pants down. In the north of Alaska, on the coast, a squadron of light RCAF bombers was based but we did no exercises with them, we were "babes in the woods". I found in my career during World War II that very few commanders or senior officers in the RCAF possessed the knowledge necessary to carry out a war. The RAF seemed to be the exception and it would be the case because they were fighting for their lives. All of the pilots were gung ho and in high spirits even without actual gun/bomb experience and morale was very high

Our squadron P40s were single engine aircraft with Allison inline engines and six 50 caliber machine guns. Our emergency landing strip was a beach on the coast, if there was any trouble. No rescue boat was available so our Mae West or life jacket plus the dingy in our seat was our only resource in case of ditching. This didn't pose much of an opportunity for survival in the very cold Pacific.

Salmon fishing was our only recreation or climbing over and through old coastal gun emplacements. We were not allowed to visit the nurses at the hospital or the native people village at the north end of the island. Our trips to Ketchikan were limited but we did manage to obtain a good supply of coffee, sugar and, of course, liquor, which was very limited on our base. Pete Wilson and Jack Bairns kept a close eye on us as our Flight Commanders. Later, both Pete and Jack were killed in Europe.

P40 aircraft

The difference between the P40 and the Hurricane is that the Hurricane was basically built by the austere British and the pilot's convenience was kept to a minimum and the plane's performance was kept to a maximum. It was a great airplane, hard to spin, would stall and flick out, but it had plenty of engine. While we used the

Allison engine in Bagotville, these had Merlin engines. The Kitty Hawk was an American fighter with an Allison engine with a cockpit that was fairly large and comfortable, while the Hurricane's cockpit was crowded but very functional. The Americans were great for electrical switches. I think we had 52 switches on the P40 when we started the aircraft, which made it very difficult if you were on a scramble or alert situation.

The Hurricane used the Merlin engine which was as powerful engine as the Allison but the P40 was a bit slower to work with given the heaviness of the plane. The Hurricane was designed to be patched up and returned to service as quickly as possible, while the P40 had metal skin throughout and was harder to work with.

When we were told we were being transferred to Sea Island, British Columbia we were very excited. We rounded up our ground crew who were shipped out early to set up the receiving area. You remember it was Alaska, which is in the American sphere, so we had plenty of sugar, coffee, tea and liquor. I asked the crew chief if it would be transferred and he laughed and said it has already been done. I presumed that he looked after his supply of liquor and he made sure I could bring out the coffee, tea and sugar for my family. The bombs and bullets were pushed into the bog where they vanished into the quicksand and the planes were loaded with food stuffs.

Flying in formation down the inland passage we saw a shape like a submarine but it turned out to be a whale so everyone relaxed, especially the Commanding Officer, I could just see his report--attacked enemy submarine with coffee and sugar--sank same. We were supposedly an operational squadron, ready to do battle, never having practiced with the guns in our planes or dropped a bomb. This is what I mean about our senior officers not knowing the first thing about war.

Formation Flying

SEA ISLAND –
VANCOUVER, BRITISH COLUMBIA

ON THE 5ᵀᴴ OF AUGUST, 1943, WE FORMED THE SQUADRON OVER Annette Island and headed south to Sea Island. We flew tight formation all the way down and when we flew over Vancouver we were told to give them an airshow. We formed up wingtip-to-wingtip with about forty P40s. It was quite a sight and a great deal of noise! Radio silence between aircraft was in effect at all times so we communicated with each other using hand signals, thus the need to fly close together. IF we wanted someone to fly behind us we hit the back of our neck so we all took position one behind the other. If we were turning right, you signaled accordingly, this included climbing and diving.

We were kept on alert 24/7 to protect something, we knew not what. We slept in the plane area, with our clothes on ready to take our planes over Vancouver Island as a show of force. We would always scramble at dawn to fight the elusive enemy. The fact that our planes had no ammunition and we didn't know how to fire our guns was never given any thought by the brains at Headquarters.

We made quite a nuisance of ourselves flying over tour boats and waving at the passengers, our planes a few hundred feet over the water, that was protecting the island. On one of the formation flying trips, ground crew phoned to tell me my wife Ethel had given birth to a daughter, Sandra Elizabeth Hilton, on August 21, 1943 in Lethbridge. I was a shaky new father landing my airplane that day and calling my wife on the telephone.

On one of our dawn patrols we intercepted a low flying Ventura aircraft who identified themselves as friendly, of course. While we were out there my flying partner and I went sight-seeing up to Tuxedo Island, north of Vancouver. They had a big rock quarry there and we went down low to look at the quarry, watching the people above us on the ledge. We returned to Vancouver, mission accomplished, of course. It turned out that my cousin was a manager of the rock quarry and when I phoned my aunt she asked me if we had been flying up at the rock quarry on Tuxedo Island. Of course I said yes, we wanted to take a look. She told me that we had scared the living daylights out of everyone there, they hit the deck because they thought it was an air raid and they were scared stiff. She said she thought I might have had a hand in it. I told her we had just been sightseeing and having fun.

While on leave in Stirling, Alberta where I met my new daughter, in August, 1943 we were told that the Squadron was going to be sent overseas and we were getting a new designation, 438th Squadron. I was ordered back to Sea Island to report to the new Squadron and my father-in-law flagged down a train, put me on the caboose and wired ahead to hold the train going from Calgary to Vancouver so I could get back to Sea Island! Pays to know people, I guess.

It took three to four days to go by rail to Halifax so I took my wife Ethel and our new daughter to Toronto for a combined farewell-- a disastrous decision! My father got us involved in a car accident and I had to leave Ethel with one black eye and a cut lip. She went back to Stirling, Alberta to sit out the war in a C.P.R. station with her mother and father, while I caught a train to Halifax. I was lucky to have such generous and pleasant in-laws as my family in Toronto were not the type to step into the breach.

My wife Ethel and daughter Sandra

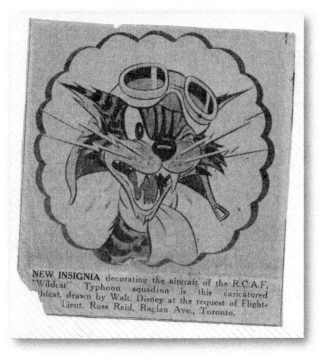

NEW INSIGNIA decorating the aircraft of the R.C.A.F. "Wildcat" Typhoon squadron is this caricatured ldcat, drawn by Walt. Disney at the request of Flight-Lieut. Ross Reid, Raglan Ave., Toronto.

Insignia designed by Disney employee for 438ᵗʰ Squadron

Official insignia sewn on uniforms

HALIFAX, BOURNEMOUTH– 438TH SQUADRON

OUR 438TH SQUADRON ARRIVED IN HALIFAX AND WE WERE assigned barracks. We were the same Squadron members from Annette Island and Sea Island so we knew each other. In the military it is wise to be friendly with everyone, but not too friendly-just keep it simple. We were told not to phone, considering security, etc. etc. The day we were to load on the transport we were paraded, with a military band, in daylight through the streets of Halifax into our transport--the Mauritania, sister ship of the Lusitania and the first operational Squadron from Canada climbed on board. It gave me cold chills. None of us had fired our aircraft guns or dive-bombed a target. We were well trained in flying but lacking in fighting skills and using our weapons. Poor leadership from the top and lack of operational knowledge were letting boys being sent to do a man's job trained in the use of a fly-swatter.

Leaving Halifax in daylight was an experience. To see the submarine nets open wide for us to reach the mouth of the Halifax Harbour made us feel like naked babies. The ship surged out at full speed and commenced a zig-zag pattern. She had 5,000 troops on board and lifeboats for 3,000 so I suppose 2,000 were assumed to be swimmers. Meals on a troop ship are served on a scheduled time twice a day and the bunks were 12 feet high, just like the Ritz. Some days we saw icebergs and other days we soaked in the sun on the deck. It took ten days to reach Liverpool where we were loaded on a train, at night, with all blinds drawn--blackout. We had some aircraft using us as a dummy targets. They flew over us at 90 knots, I think they were Tiger Moths. We were concerned that we'd be fighting a war with that equipment. When we saw the light of day we were in Bournemouth in the south of England.

When we arrived, we were put into a hotel and our first breakfast was quite an occasion. We had English cooks and it left a lot to be desired but it was wartime and you took what you could get. We were lined up for breakfast and were greeted with this concoction called Bubble and Squeak--a mixture of potatoes and brussel sprouts all fried together in one hell of a mess. We also got black bread. When Roy Bern went up to the line cook and asked for a piece of white toast, she looked at him like he'd lost his mind and slapped a piece of black bread on his plate. Bubble and Squeak followed us everywhere we went and I can tell you there's nothing more uncomfortable than diving bombing from 20,000 ft to 5,000 ft with your stomach full of cabbage and potatoes, it makes for a very pressurized situation.

We practiced a lot of low level flying because that was going to be our role in the future. Flying only Hurricanes had given us lots of experience. One of our pilots said he always knew where to land because he would see the red roofs of the village. We told him all the villages had red roofs. Poor guy, he probably got lost a lot. On one of his trips he came in and collided with one of the pillboxes so we asked him why he hadn't gone around? He said he had to go to the bathroom and that's when we told him that's what the high boots were for. We did a lot of low level flying, and I mean low level. We were told not to scare the cattle in the field.

WELLINGFORD LINCOLN—ENGLAND

NOVEMBER AND EARLY DECEMBER OUR SQUADRON WHICH WAS now called 438th Squadron was sent to Digby to fly Hurricane aircraft from a small field at Wellingore Lincoln. We staged around a grass strip which had a strip of oil on it to simulate a runway.. It was surrounded by concrete pill boxes which Flying Officer Booker, a pilot who marched to his own drummer, managed to bend a Hurricane over the concrete dome. Just pride was damaged, as well as the aircraft.

Next stop for our Squadron was December 19 to RAF Station Wittering in Wellingore, which is just outside of Winchester, England. Here we were exposed to the real RAF mess, complete with a butler to serve us. We Canadians had to be on our best behavior. We used to sit around the living area, listening to the record player, with a local girl Alice, as our waitress. She had a habit of putting her thumb in the soup when she carried the bowls to us but we ate the soup anyway. She was the daughter of the local lord of the manor, and she was doing her

war duty to help the cause. A squadron of Spitfires with the clipped
wing model, were also stationed here making sweeps over France.

Canadian Pilots trying to look like we belong

We went out and bought out the little black bicycles with no lights
and we'd ride into Wellingore to the local pub and sit around, play
darts with the locals. I remember Hutchinson and I went in one time
and the police constable was always chasing us because we had no
lights. We would scatter into different directions in the total black
night, get home and put our bikes away.

We had a Squadron Leader from the desert who had been ordered to teach us how to low fly. It was like candy to a kid for we crazy Canadians so he took us out, told us to take off, drop down to 6 feet after you raise your wheels, and fly over the cows in the fields. You should be past them before the noise scares them. Out in the water, there were fishing boats and sail boats, and we did the same to them

AYRE, SCOTLAND – TYPHOONS

WE FLEW UP TO AYR, SCOTLAND ON JANUARY 13, 1944 FLYING OUR Hurricanes, where the Typhoons were delivered by women of the Auxiliary RAF for us. Why we went to Scotland to pick up planes delivered to us from England? Who knows? The difference between a Typhoon and a Hurricane was unbelievable! The Typhoon landed at 110 mph with a runway of 2500 ft. with a pilot standing on the brakes. You had to make sure you undershot, but not too far! You made your turn coming into approach at 120, slowing it down to 110. God knows what the stall rate was. One of our pilots took the Typhoon up to 30,000 ft and put it into a spin. It took him almost the complete 30,000 to get it out of that spin because it was so heavy. He got it out of the spin at 4,000 ft landed white as a ghost and told us to never spin the Typhoon which we never did. The plane was loaded with plated armour underneath and a Napier Sabre engine which was a 24 cylinder liquid cooled engine with four 20mm cannons, capable of carrying two 500 lb bombs or two 1,000 lb bombs. The aircraft required the pilot to be awake and it had torque to burn. If you didn't get the airstream over the tail it would take off across the field. The pilot flew this plane constantly; there was no sitting back and just riding along. We had no crashes with the Typhoon and I can't honestly say why--maybe we paid more attention given its idiosyncratic behavior. When you are flying formation, you are busy, flying in concert with another, and you have to adjust to each movement of every person in the squadron. if you're the leader it's not so bad, they had to line up on you, but it always needed adjusting. You're working all the time.

We were checked out on the aircraft by a factory representative pointing out the starting procedures, flap levels, undercarriage, throttle, gas and other features. After a few minutes of him peering into the cockpit and explaining all the goodies his departing comment was "don't lower the flaps for the air cooler over 220 mph". That gave me the confidence to taxi out and try this beast. When I opened the throttle I imagined I was going to be sitting on the tail. I took off and it was a case of the blind leading the blind. It took me two times around the airport to slow it down to the landing speed of 110 mph. Our old Hurricanes' top airspeed could barely reach 110mph! Fortunately, I remembered to lower my wheels and to my surprise made a "greaser" of a landing. First and last time! Once you got it on the ground it was like a duck, it just squatted. When you were in the air

Hawker Typhoon

you were working all the time. You did not sit back and snooze, like flying the Hurricane which was a beautiful, stable machine.

It was important to know your role in the air. Planes flew in groups of four, with one plane as the #1 and the second plane as #2 -- the wingman. The #2 plane flew beside his #1 with his wing slightly below the #1 in formation, not necessarily up close but a few feet below the wing. In the case of a sudden turn there would be room for both planes to make that change without a collision. Obviously, with the Typhoon attention to detail saved lives.

Jack Hilton with Hawker Typhoon

HERN – ENGLAND

WE WERE POSTED FOR ARMY MANEUVERS FEBRUARY 15, 1944 which brought us down closer to the Coast of France. Training, training and more training. In March I did more flying on the Typhoon practicing air to ground attack with the 20mm cannon. When I first fired them I almost ejected from the airplane, it was a horrendous feeling and the noise was unbelievable!

Finally our squadron was posted to Hern bringing Typhoons and Hurricanes down with us. We were the first operation over France. I had eight hours on the Typhoon when I was ordered to take it over to France and bomb a bridge and rail yard. It didn't seem like a lot of experience to enter combat with but we were at war so we dive-bombed from 20,000 ft, which is not what the Typhoon is designed for. It is a low-level bombing and strafing plane and it was a very long time before we a) got up to 20,000 ft, and b) formed up and c) went off to bomb.

438ᵗʰ Squadron, Jack Hilton, top row, far right

Maintenance happened wherever possible, even grassy fields

Jack Hilton, pilot, with fellow pilots and aircrew maintenance

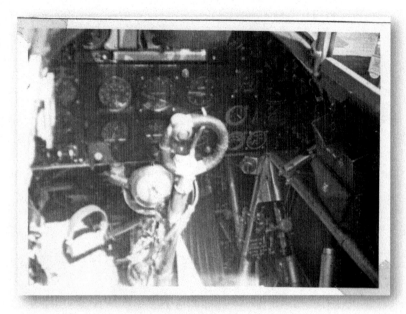

Hawker Typhoon cockpit

I was ordered to fly with the Wing Commander as #2 wingman and I was ordered not to lose him. I said I'd do my best so when he went into a dive, I was right there. He pulled up, looked over and there I was. He waved at me and I think he was trying to wave me away but I had been told not to lose the Wing Commander. He saw something down on the track so down we went-- together. Flying formation with this guy was absolutely exhausting, wherever he went, I went. When we landed it was side-by-side. We taxied up to the dispersal and he said "who the hell was my #2? I think he was trying to hit me, he wouldn't leave me alone!". I was told not to lose the Wing Commander and the Squadron leader told me "good job!" I guess I stayed too close.

We contacted Headquarters in London and asked for a bombing range and we were given a map for reference. We all gathered around and looked at the map reference which turned out to be the coast of France, so that's what we did. We did formation flying, bombing and strafing with the Typhoons and we did what we called GCC control. That was two of us flying over the clouds, we were radar controlled from the ground and were on a timed run into the target. We began counting down from 10 and as soon as we reached that we pushed the button and got rid of two 500 lb bombs.

On April 12 we attacked a German target which shot off the flying bombs. It was a series of ramps and sled-type equipment that would shoot off the buzz bombs, which were little 500 lb bombs with a jet engine, more or less. Unbeknownst to the Wing Commander we would tip the buzz bomb with our wing and sent it back to the Germans. Since this was never condoned this action was never recorded in log books.

Several years after the war I was reading a book about airplane cockpits and learned--for the first time--that the Typhoon's cockpit filled with carbon monoxide the entire time the engine was on. No one told any of us this useful piece of information and I am sure it contributed to many deaths. I was at 20,000 ft heading for a railway line when my cockpit filled with a red glow. I felt warm and peaceful, something I had never felt before--or since. I took my hands off the stick and it nosed straight down dropping to 5,000 ft before I reached for the stick and pulled it up. When I went back I told the doctor and he ordered me to take 10 days leave.

Bridge prior to bombing

On April 30th dive-bombing a bridge in Cherbourg, France my aircraft was hit by anti-aircraft fire but there were no problems returning home. We were kept busy over France and attacking mostly tanks, trucks and bridges but we never could catch a train.

Someone in England had the stupid idea of sending 30 Typhoons in formation. It took us forever to create formation, fly up to 30,000 ft and dive bomb. Dive bombing from 30,000 using the gun sight as a guide is not effective but, we rolled over and went down. On the count of three you pull your wing sights and let go your bombs. We dive bombed a site in LeHavre twice, on the 5th and 6th of June.

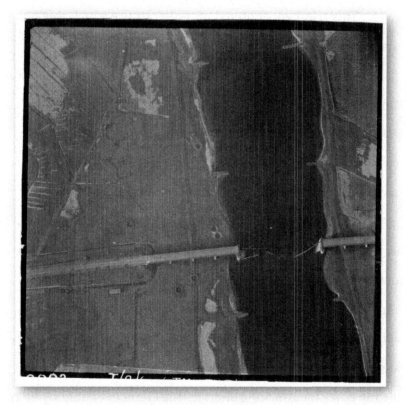

Bridge after bombing

The invasion was a shuttle service. You would take your round, return, sleep while another batch took over. We had orders from London that a certain portion of France was so controlled by the Germans that we were to shoot at everything that moved, whether it was a guy plowing a field, riding a bike, or whatever. So we did.

April 1944 saw the 438th Squadron attack in France carrying 500 lb bombs on various targets such as ship convoys on the French coast, viaducts at Bolbeck, France and submarine pens at Cherbourg, France. This trip I encountered anti-aircraft fire which was quite accurate but was able to bring us home.

The week of June 14th we worked over the bridges at Bremmer, Samson and Chard. We dive-bombed from 10,000 ft to 5,000 ft and took out the bridge at Canne. When you air attack, you are gone. You don't really see what you've done, you don't know if you were successful or not--it was a hit and run situation.

438th Squadron now formed with 439th and 440th Squadron. The last two squadrons carried rockets with 25 lb warheads with the firepower of a light cruiser. Now we were 143rd RCAF Wing.

In June 1944 several bridges near Cannes were attacked by our typhoons and we also did radar controlled bombing runs through clouds. On June 27th, we attacked a train, where our job was to provide top cover for attacking aircraft. The Germans would set up traps to catch planes strafing trains. One train we attacked, four of us came in right on the trees at 100 ft off the ground in single file. As we came in the box car sides of the train fell away and we were facing flak guns. I fired as I went by, going over and down below the trees. The guns have a stop on them and can only go so low, but others were not as lucky. The squadron leader pullled up short and had the tail of his plane blown off. Luckily he was able to make it home. That was one terrifying experience, looking down the muzzles of multiple anti-aircraft guns and the Germans were happy to see us coming.

Fortunately for me I had more experience behind me because I was an instructor. When I went overseas I had more flying hours than anyone else in my squadron and that's what kept me alive. I didn't do stupid things because I had learned through experience that you did not go around a second time--you did the run and then you got the hell out of there.

We all knew an invasion was coming because of the ground activity of tanks and armour filling southern England. It's a wonder the island didn't sink from the weight of it all. We were all confined to camp prior to June 6, 1944 and that was a major clue something big was going to happen. June 6 arrived and we were told the invasion was on. Our aircraft were painted with white stripes on the underside, in theory to provide identification as Allied aircraft. We slept in tents on the ground next to our aircraft. It was a dull, rainy day with low cloud cover and we were told the ceiling was about 1800 ft. After a lousy breakfast consisting of tea, four of us took off to provide support by flying top cover over loading crafts. The channel was a sight to behold with boats and ships covering most of the water. Our job was to provide top cover for the Canadian troops going ashore on Juno beach, attack coastal guns that were sunk into the cliffs and cover the troops as they landed. We fired our four 20mm guns at the

Germans to force them to keep their heads down and then skipped the 500 lb bombs at the guns pulling up afterwards to fly above the cliffs--at about 200 ft. Passing over the landing crafts we could see the infantry running up the beaches into France. Our height was about 1,000 ft so the view was perfect while the soldiers were dealing with choppy waves, constant bombardment and a requirement to walk waist deep in water onto the beach. The bad weather was a handicap to getting enough altitude to do a proper bombing mission but we did the best we could.

After dropping our bombs our formation of four Typhoons swept further inland and attacked a German truck convoy moving up to the landing area where we did a tremendous amount of damage. Then we returned to base to catch some rest as another pilot took the plane out and once it returned, I went back out. Repeat as necessary. I wasn't sure when the bullet hit the wing but the hole left no mistake that the plane had been hit. Thankfully, it had minimal effect.

One time when a loaner RAF ground crew member was strapping me in to take my flight, the tea wagon came by. He stopped everything to jump down and get tea. I yelled at him to get back and finish his job, we had a war to win!! He was one seriously annoyed Brit, but he did come back and finish the job.

My regular ground crew decided, one day, to take a mixture of gasoline and kerosene, wash down the plane and then polish it to a high shine. Once finished, they asked me to take it up and see if it made any difference...which I did. When I landed I told them their work had added an additional 5-10 mph to the plane's speed and congratulated them on their initiative!!

At that time we were buying motorcycles, we all had them wherever we could get them. Mine cost me $50. When I brought it back to base I realized I didn't know how to turn it off so, wise me, I figured I would run it around until it ran out of gas. Well that wasn't going to happen any time soon, so finally I laid it on its side to run its heart out and I went to bed.

Finally General Montgomery ordered all air crew to cease riding motorcycles--too many injuries, broken arms, etc. and it was impacting the war effort. We could fly 525 mph in an airplane but not manage motorcycles!

My motorcycle

My most wonderful motorcycle

Returning from a bombing run

We were in pretty good shape in England regarding bathhouses, or showers. They were available to us with hot water, if we put money into the machine, but the moment we left England to go to France, our sanitary conditions never reached a high standard. We lived in tents, our airfields were portable, and we were constantly in motion so our health conditions weren't good. We had outside privies and we had no hot water so we would cut one of the gas cans in half, filling one with sand, and the other was filled with water. We would put gasoline into the can full of sand and light it, and it would create the heat necessary to warm the water for washing and shaving. It was very limited and didn't allow for washing clothes, and shower facilities were not available, We shaved daily as the rubber oxygen masks did not do well with the hair on unshaven faces.

The cooks worked out of the trucks so our food was based on what was available. In England we had brussel sprouts, potatoes and black bread with the occasional Spam and bologna. For 10 shillings, when we were in London, we got horse steak, potatoes and a glass of milk and that was a luxury but on the continent we had no washing facilities, no showers, even though the Army had portable showers and the Red Cross never showed up in our units.

We didn't have extra clothes to change into, no way to wash the clothes we had, so life was very primitive. We were dirty and we were hungry but then everyone else was too so it didn't matter. The rations in Europe were black bread, powdered eggs, reconstituted sausages which were filled with everything under the sun, and most of it indescribable.

June 1944 was a busy month with fighter sweeps into France to support the army. On one of our trips we encountered three ME190 German fighters, fortunately Spitfires arrived to chase them off. This was fortunate because our idiot Squadron Leader had us returning with 2,500 lbs each and we were directly over British Royal Navy ships who were shelling the beachhead in support of the landing. Ships do not take kindly to aircraft dropping bombs on them and that is what we would have had to do if the German fighters had attacked

Coming back from a sweep over France, four of us came upon a Lancaster that was shot full of holes and smoking and we automatically surrounded him to keep enemy fighters away and also to note if he landed in the water for air/sea rescue. He made it back to the White Cliffs of Dover, and we escorted him as he landed. They had paved the top of the cliffs for planes to land on, it was a huge landing strip. 24 aircraft could take off side-by- side. We landed with the Lancaster bomber and we walked over and walked around it. We heard this tremendous swearing so we went to the back area where the gunner --whose gun had been sheared off like a knife through butter-- his turret had been swung right around, facing forward and was jammed in that position. His tailbone was sitting out in the slip-stream all the way back from Berlin and boy, was he one mad person. We stood and laughed at him which he didn't appreciate that, but then we helped him out of the turret down onto the ground and boy, was he ever cold! The whole crew landed successfully, even with frost-bite. We took off and went back to our base at Hern.

One day we were told to stand down for three or four days, probably to save fuel. I decided to use the leave to go up to York because a friend of mine from Toronto, Bert Scrimger had called. He and I had grown up as little kids together and our parents were friends. His parents had been best man and maid of honor at my parents' wedding so we go a long way back and we lived side by side in Scarborough, Ontario. His grandmother called him Burkie, which is Gaelic for fighter, and that he was. He was a miserable little kid and we used to fight with each other regularly.

He was stationed with a bomber squadron up in York so I got a couple of sandwiches and headed up by train to York. I swung in to see my friend, he was in the orderly room at the time and it was kind of a stir to have an officer come and call on a Corporal. Everybody was in awe as Bert introduced me around as his friend from Scarborough who was with a Fighter Squadron. Bomber Command and Fighter Command are two different things so everybody was asking me questions. We went over to his quarters, they were in double-bunks and he asked me to stay. When we discussed where we were going to eat, I told him to give me his tunic so I could dine with him and the other Corporals. He went to work during the day and I goofed around a bit, then I went back to Hern.

Another time I had a few days off in England again so I went up to York, discovered he'd been promoted to Sergeant, so I got to eat in the Sergeants mess and had a great time with all of his friends. I was just getting ready to leave, and along came the Barrack Officer. Bert introduced him to me and he said well you should be over in the officer's mess. Bert said hey, he's a friend of mine, he came to eat with me. I didn't see him again until we were back in Canada after the war.

One time four of us, Pete Wilson, Jack Barnes, myself and George White were flying over the English Channel to the coast of France into an area that was flooded. We took off in the dusk, which isn't smart as we were not night fighters. We had no exhaust suppressors, and the exhaust becomes very predominant and bits of carbon are being thrown out. In a fighter aircraft you are sitting right next to the engine so we crossed over to the coast of France with bits of carbon thrown back at us. We flew in the finger formation, which is four planes, each stepped down from the other, with me flying fourth. When you are flying over water it is very difficult to pick out targets, but we could see the anti-aircraft fire coming out of Calais, so we went in to the target. Pete Wilson rolled over, his #2 went with him and I was following the #3 man and down we went into our dive. As the fourth man down, diving into water at dusk I couldn't see anything but black water and I lost the whole crowd so I went down, dropped my bombs and when I looked up I saw four Typhoons headed to Calais. I climbed up to join them briefly, but saw they were headed to

Calais and I didn't want to go back so I turned back to England.

We had radio system where we punched a button for a homing device. So I radioed "Victor Charlie, english to base". A nice little English lady came on the line, repeated my call sign, and told me to do a 90 degree turn to the right for identification , which I did. She said yes I have you on contact on radar so steer o 9 o to base and she tells me my base is 120 miles at 12 o'clock. I held the course she gave me and she brought me right over, told me I was there and they had been notified I was coming and be prepared to land. They turned on the landing lights and boy, was it a beautiful sight. As I touched down, they turned the lights off which made it like landing into a bag. I kept going straight until I ran out of speed so I phoned the tower and told them to send someone out to tow me in to dispersal, which they did. I kept thinking there must be a German fighter on my tail just waiting.

On one of our sweeps over France, we were led by Wing Commander Davidson who had just come back from the Far East and he had engine trouble so he had to land in France. We circled above him to keep the Germans away from him while one of our planes landed in a field next to him. The Wing Commander pushed the destruct button for his damaged airplane, the rescue pilot threw his parachute out to make room for the Wing Commander and they flew home with him sitting on the pilot's lap.

FRANCE – B/5 AND B/6 STRIPS

ON JUNE 27ᵀᴴ, OUR SQUADRON WAS INSTRUCTED TO LAND IN France at a strip called B-6. This was a metal strip laid down under a wheat field and had several revetments for our aircraft to use as parking areas. A revetment was an area surrounded by sandbags which provided room for the planes to taxi in and turn around. This protected the planes from enemy aircraft machine gunning them or anti-aircraft or even rifle fire. The sandbags were higher than the air-planes and called revetments.

Our trucks with ground crew, supplies and mess tents had been ferried over prior to our landing. The metal surface was very uneven and very short, about 5,000 ft in length. To land an aircraft such as the Typhoon which landed at 110 mph was an indication of our skills. An idiot Squadron leader took the squadron in a left hand circuit prior to landing which took us right over the front lines. At 110 mph, with wheels and flaps down, my aircraft took a German bullet in the wing. We were directed to our parking spaces by our crew and after turning off my engine, I opened the top only to have a sniper bullet pass behind my head. To say I moved like a worm leaving the aircraft would be correct. Our stay at B-6 was short as we deployed to B-5 strip; much the same, but without sniper bullets.

We lived in tents and were constantly deluged with anti-aircraft debris. Most of us dug slit trenches in our tents so we could go underground to sleep with our metal helmets on.

One night we heard a German plane come over--we could tell it was a German plane because its engines weren't synchronized and they threw up a lot of flak. We greeted the German with anti-aircraft guns and gunners on ships off shore. I don't think we got him, but the flying shrapnel kept us awake and on our toes. We weren't very well rested, we weren't very well fed, we were dirty, couldn't wash with water, no change of clothes and no one to do our laundry but we all stuck it out since we had no choice.

We were living in tents, so the Officers Mess got together, pooled some money and send it over to England for beer. The theory was we'd get the lining from two drop tanks which we used for extra flying hours and we'd fly them back to England and one of our chaps would purchase the beer, load the drop tanks and fly it back. We picked probably the least reliable guy in the unit, by the name of Hutchinson. He was a hail-fellow-well met kind of guy, utterly unreliable. Off he goes to England and time passes. When he landed back on base, he told us that he had the liners onboard, full of beer, but accidentally hit the eject button and they both fell into the English Channel. Of course not one of us believed him, but gone was our money, gone was our beer and gone was the opportunity to drink away some of France's dust.

When I went on leave back to England, I spent time with a very distant relative and the two of us would sit and read paperback books. Once I was promoted to an officer, I was able to stay at the Officer's Club in London where I would eat and sleep the night, during the day I would take my raincoat and lay it on the grass in parks and sleep the day away. When I returned to my Squadron, stories of great parties and wild activities ensued, but in reality, sleep was the greatest gift I could give myself. I always wondered about those that told the party stories when they came back from leave!

A couple of days after D-Day we were assigned to harass German support coming up to fight. At one point the Canadians had broken through. The German's were just about surrounded at Chalet's Gap, if we closed the gap we would have captured the whole German army defending France. Our air support for troops going forward caught Germans retreating up the country roads. They were firing at us, we fired back, and it was a fighter's dream when you come down overtop transport being pulled by horses, tanks moving at a slow speed and piled up with German troops sitting on them. The Typhoons were ideal for this sort of thing and we were strafing the roads before and after to try to hurry them back to Germany—we were very success-ful. You only have about 2-3 minutes of ammunition so you had to be careful not to run out of bullets and still do an effective job on the tanks, troops, trucks and cannons, It was quite a mess. We didn't close the gap but we sure made an inroad on the casualty part of the German army.

One day I came in from a sweep and taxied into my parking area and the engine was running rough, so I swung around, put the brakes on and opened the throttle testing my switches. My crew chief was standing beside the wing while I did all this, and with the sand all around us blowing up a storm the crew chief was killing himself laughing. He pointed over my shoulder to my left where there was a bank of bathrooms with sheets of burlap to give a little privacy. With the engine roaring, the burlap was straight out. This poor air-man, with his pants down around him, his hat blown off and his hair straight up holding onto the toilet seat right in the middle of this slip-stream. I shut the engine down and apologized to the poor airman.

July saw us receiving daily visits at night from German night fight-ers and the fireworks from our anti-aircraft guns were better than holiday fireworks. Of course the shrapnel fell on our tents so again we slept when we could with our tin helmets on our heads.

Our role was as close support so we ground fired into German po-sitions by having us fly behind the front lines and receive a call from a forward army observer. This is called CAD rank and it gave good support to the Canadian troops. Our firing and bombing would be about 1,000 yards ahead of the Canadians. The troops fired yellow smoke artillery shells into the position they wanted us to attack, covering their positions with coloured fluorescent sheets. It worked very well!

We used to fly one day, and then have a half day off. On our day off 3 or 4 of us took a jeep and went up to the front lines. We drove into this group of Canadian soldiers on the side of the road in a field and I was walking along and there was a guy blackening up his face and I said "my god, Dunbar" a high school friend. We sat and talked about home, food, girls, it's fairly constant as to what people talk about when they meet someone from home and then he said "how are you eating, Jack?". I said we're eating the biscuits and rehydrated sausages, the usual bullybeef and brussel sprouts. I asked him what he was eating, he said "chicken, beef, and we take them from all the bombed out houses". He took me to a field and there was a French chateau, with a big lawn and a bunch of cows. He said he'd put them in protective custody, about 15-20 cows and he asked if I'd like any meat. I said sure so they shot the cow, dressed it out, and put it on the jeep. Back we go to the airfield with the goodies and made everyone happy eating fresh meat. The dysentry was pretty horrific given the toilets were cans out in the field and all of a sudden we're all rushing around searching for empty cans The whole Squadron was immobilized. We enjoyed the beef and paid the price.

On one of our other days off, my friend Vince McMann and I

hitched a ride on an ambulance to the front to see what the war looked like from the front trenches. When we got there, the Germans were shooting off Moaning Minnie mortars that would fire in rotation and it sounded like a moaning, wailing sound. Vince and I huddled under a gun carrier and the guy said you're crazy coming up when you don't have to, so we told him we had a half day off with nothing much to do. We wandered back and got into a first aid station and the doctor said you guys look like you're suffering from nervous tension--what you need is a glass of rum. Well we were both non-drinkers, but he gave us a glass full of 110 proof navy rum. We looked at each other, put the glass under our nose but we couldn't drink it..so the doctor drank it. The Germans cut the road off so we were stuck at the first aid station

The Canadian troops cleared the road and we rode back in the ambulance, with patients. The Squadron Leader gave us hell for going up into the war zone and said you're no good to us dead so stay home. We didn't do it again.

This happened when we were transferring from one green field to another green field in France where our ground crew had gone ahead and the metal strips had been laid down to land on. We came in one at a time to land and one of the chaps, Flying Officer Frizette was following us in and he was making his turn. It was a continuous turn from 500 ft into the runway, gauging your landing to come across the runway. When he started to round out for his landing run, the local anti-aircraft gunners decided to use him as a target as he was coming in to land. He landed but he was most definitely hostile. He taxied in, jumped out, drew his revolver and he was heading off to every anti-aircraft position to feel the barrels for warmth to see what s.o.b. had shot at him. We had to restrain him to keep him from shooting somebody.

On New Year's day 1944, I was down on the flight line when the German air force with Messerschmidts 109s and 190s came across our airfield with no prior warning. Our anti-aircraft guns were caught unprepared and were ineffective. Pete Wilson was taxiing out with a Typhoon. He tried to take off, but he didn't make it, another casualty of war. As they were strafing everyone, I jumped into a bomb hole to get out of the way. It was full of icy water so I'm up to my neck in freezing water, but it was better than being Pete Wilson, caught unaware on the runway.

BELGIUM –
RAF 193ᴿᴰ TYPHOON SQUADRON

THEN THE RAF PUT OUT A CALL FOR TYPHOON PILOTS AND I WAS sent to a holding Squadron in England and this made for a nice holiday from the war. No doubt I was chosen as I had a slight difference of opinion with a replacement Squadron Leader in our RCAF unit- -another idiot. Flying every day, getting shot at coming and doing, with bad food, poor sleep and primitive living conditions, we were all short tempered and edgy. This cocky little Squadron Leader was a drinker, and he and I met in the Officer's tent where I was drinking orange pop. He came up to me and told me I needed to drink more, at which point I told him it was none of his damn business and that didn't go over too well. He ordered me off the base so I got into an air/ sea rescue boat and went over to England to Warrington, which is a holding unit for the RCAF. I met Wing Commander Johnny Johnson,

95

our fighter pilot ace. He asked me what the heck I was doing there, and I told him that I had told the Squadron Leader to go to hell. Wing Commander told me to go over to the RAF who were short of pilots so they transferred me into their unit

On October,1944 my ferry aircraft carried us to my new Squadron, 193rd Typhoon Squadron, Antwerp, Belgium. The aircraft took a slight detour over the German-held Dunkirk area at 500 ft doing about 110 mph. The German anti-aircraft guns welcomed us by shooting out our starboard engine forcing us to crash land in a field. We had our parachutes with us but we were too low so we didn't jump--what comes, comes. Most of us just looked at each other and shrugged. A perfect crash landing in yet another farmer's field and we were picked up by the army and delivered to 193rd Fighter Squadron RAF safely

The next day I spent time getting settled in my new bombed-out apartment.

We pulled down picket fences and the odd telephone pole for heat and cooking materials.

I sent one of the aides off to round up a 45 gallon drum and he rolled it down the bombed out street and put it under the apartment. We cut the top off, put it on top of bricks and built up a fire base for this barrel of water, and pretty soon we had hot water. It was very popular with everyone -- they came down to get hot water to shave. There was an old box spring in a bombed out house and I told the guys to haul it back to my room to make my sleeping bed more comfortable. You had to be creative, like camping out only in Europe in cities.

We were under constant fire from V1s and V2s which you would hear after they had hit.

One day I was standing at this one window we had left and just as I turned around a bomb went off and the window shattered, covering my back with glass. While I'm brushing myself off and thanking my lucky stars, bombs hit the huge gas storage tanker and the downtown movie theater with 800 people inside. I have no idea how many, if any, survived.

One morning our squadron was given a briefing from Group headquarters to attack a target with a map reference. There were 24 of us with 500 lb bombs and we gathered around Wing Commander Davidson, a very fine chap, battle hardened and not prepared to take any guff even from headquarters. It was a bridge we were after, surrounded by anti-aircraft sites. Group headquarter suggested we dive bomb from 10,000 ft to 5,000 ft and it didn't matter to us but the Wing Commander looked at the map , saw the target and the anti-aircraft guns around it with the anti-aircraft guns all in red. This map had a solid red silhouette to it. He picked up the phone and called Headquarters and asked "who is the idiot who designed this mission into this area?". When they told him he suggested the planning officers come over and join the Squadron and ride along. He told them that if the target was attacked per their orders, over 50%

of them wouldn't come home, and if you people in Group think 12 trained pilots and 12 aircraft are worth it, come along and share the ride. Call me back, once you've evaluated the value of the target. We heard much yelling and cursing and he hung up on them and we applauded. He said "there's no bloody way anyone is coming back from that target". The phone rang again and the mission was scrubbed. We all breathed a sigh of relief.

We supported the invasion of Walchem Island in Holland and it was over a lot of flooded country. November is a bad month for weather, rain and snow, giving very low ceiling for aircraft flying. Our job was to attack heavy gun positions at Flushing and German troops at Tonnenkrech, Holland. Roads and railways also came under our consideration doing extensive damage to German communications positions.

On November 11 our squadron was sent to cut rail lines near Goth and the strangest aircraft flew suddenly through our formation, it was on fire and had no propellers. Welcome to our first jet fighter. It had limited range so it kept on going. Next day we set two Typhoons up into the sun above us and when he tried the same tactic he did not return to base.

November 25, eight Typhoons were sent into Holland to attack the German airfield. The new Flight Lieutenant RCAF Hilton was among the eight. As the Battle of the Bulge was on and Brussells was threatened, we were to attack aircraft on the ground. Inbound, two

Typhoons developed trouble so they and their wing men returned to base, leaving four Typhoons to do the job.

We were flying at 8,000 ft and saw below several tight formations of German aircraft. They looked like a cluster of bees around a queen bee. With about 50 bees below us, air cover was blown, so we just dove through this formation catching them by surprise. i have never seen so many black crosses in my life. With the numbers against us we were wise to make one pass, firing our cannon as we dove through. it must have upset their timing over the battlefield as they were well scattered. We drove right down to the deck and flew home at 500 mph, better a live coward than a dead hero. The weather was very poor with low visibility, rain and snow.

A combination of fatigue, poor food and wind sheer on landing carried my plane into a bomb hole beside the runway--sheering off the wheels and sending my aircraft end over end. The ambulance caught up with me running down the runway with three broken ribs. The driver asked me where I was going and my reply was as far away from gasoline and ammunition as I could get and don't forget the hot engine. The driver suggested I swing on board the ambulance as it was possible he could make better time. The ride to the Brussels hospital was rough on the cobbled streets, but after a short stay the ambulance drivers gave me a ride back flying fighter escort over Holland, attacking V2 rocket sites to fill up the day's activities.

Poor visibility that saved our lives

In 1945 they had #193 RAF Squadron carry out bridge and troop attacks over Holland. on one occasion we carried 1,000 lb bombs which meant single aircraft take-off and very slow climb. The going down from altitude was fast!

February 1945 our squadron, busy with interdiction, caught and destroyed an ME109 who ventured near the airdrome just as four of our Typhoons were in the circuit over the field. We all took a crack at him and he stayed with us, buried within the airfield. The ME109 was rebuilt by our ground crew and they asked me if I would take it up for a flight. I told them I'd be happy to do that if they would be so kind as to blackout the German swastika.

Downed German ME109

Ground crew working on German aircraft

Ground crew who successfully rebuilt German ME109

Me being asked to fly the rebuilt ME109

March, 1945 on taking off with 1,000 lb bombs under each wing my engine could not deliver full power so I jettisoned the bombs. One bomb would not cooperate and exploded at about 500 ft cutting my hydraulic lines so--no wheels, no flaps, just me and an engine. The airfield had laid soft sand beside the runway so I put my aircraft down safely. that was March 22. A new Typhoon was delivered to me on 23 March, go, and sin no more. Bridges trains and truck bombings continued. One of our brilliant senior officers came up with a terrific operational plan. The plan was for paratroopers to drop prior to the opening fire. Our job was to fly at 1800 ft over the anti-aircraft positions in Germany prior to the drop. Straight and level in pairs to draw fire. When seeing the bursts we were to dive at the gun pits with 500 lb bombs made up of 25 cluster bombs. The idiot that thought of this strategy had never flown aircraft at 1800 ft and pulled it out of a dive without hitting the shot from the anti-aircraft guns, but only one of the aircraft suffered damage which was a basic miracle.

Bombing SS Headquarters in Belgium

Each Squadron and each Wing had an intelligence officer, whose job it was to send information from Group Headquarters for bombing instructions. They told us about the SS headquarters, gave us directions and what they wanted done.

One of the more pleasant parts of our flying was destroying the headquarters of the hated SS. They were situated in a Dutch farm house built in a square. We had delayed fuses on our bombs and flew down the streets of the little village where we could almost read the street signs. All eight Typhoons put their bombs right down the chimney and when checking our work, a row of bricks were all that was left.

April 1945 was a busy month for the Squadron, hitting trains, armoured convoys and bombing a telephone communication center near Apeldoorn.

On one of our bombing runs anti-aircraft fire hit my plane and I thought it was going down. I opened the canopy and put my leg over the side, ready to jump, while watching the engine's temperature controls and holding the flight controls. The engine didn't alter so I climbed back in and flew it home. My wing mate was watching me fly this airplane with one leg over the side and when we got home he asked me what on earth I had been doing. I told him to come with me and see the aircraft. The nose of the plane had been stripped as clean as a new nickel and I was, once again, a most fortunate man as that was all the damage the plane had taken. We were both shaken by the view--it was really something!!

Obliterated SS headquarters

Returning home from a bombing run we caught sight of a Nazi plane taking pictures over Antwerp. I got in behind him and closed the distance. You get so close you can't miss--that's the only way to be successful. With 20 mm shells they knock the wings off. I waggled my wings which is universal air-speak for "surrender". If the answer is yes, the plane drops its wheels and is escorted to the airbase. This one didn't drop the wheels so I shot him out of the sky.

When you return from a mission you're good and tired, always under shellfire and all this stuff builds up. Your nerves are on edge and you're as cranky as can be, while you try to forget it's still there.

The war was ending and the Germans were emptying their prisoner-of-war camps. The troops walking down the roads were told NOT to jump into ditches because we had been given orders to fire on troops who were jumping into ditches and leaving people alone of they stayed on the road. One of these soldiers told me later that it was one of the hardest things he ever did--not jumping into cover when we flew over to strafe German troops.

While I was over in Antwerp flying with the 193rd Squadron, my good wife, Ethel Jane, in Stirling, Alberta would gather up parcels and mail them to me. The local man Gilbert Wells, who owned a little store, would save chocolate bars, hiding them from the Mounties as they came by during the war scrounging chocolate bars. He would refuse to give them to the Mounties and he used to make them mad. They were the only ones with fuel and could travel around the country and he would refuse to give the bars to them. They would try to push him around and being a stubborn englishman, he would say to hell with you Charlie, these are going overseas to men who are fighting for the country that you are driving around trying to scrounge chocolate bars. So anyway, my wife would package them up and they would come over to me and I was sure a popular guy when the mail came in--everybody would shout that Jack's got mail and they'd all gather in my room. They would let me open the parcel but that was as far as it got. She used to include puff biscuits, chocolate bars, things the RAF hadn't seen for years. We used to have a good old feast with all the pilots from the squadron gathering together and have a real party. They hadn't seen chocolate for years and years. I told them about the Mounties and we all decided the Mounties could go to hell and we would enjoy it!

At no time ever during the war, either in England, France or Holland, let alone anywhere in Canada did we see the Red Cross, Salvation Army and the Canadian Special Support people. We received no packages, no food, nothing, except for what my wife sent us, and this included Christmases. Neither did the United Church that I went to for years and years, not even a pair of socks, which would have been extremely useful then!

We were stationed near the German border on a makeshift flying field, which was nothing new in flying but the environment we were working with, eating our damn brussel sprouts, sleeping on the floors of bombed out buildings in sleeping bags. The environment was very hostile, and when I was going down the road in a jeep with another guy, we were always on the alert for saboteurs who wanted to waylay us. The jeep had a bar across the front because they used to string a wire across the road right at the driver's neck level and take out the windshield and driver. One of the trips I was with a driver and we were going up to headquarters, and there were 4 youths standing beside the road, with fists clenched in a hand grenade attitude with their arm behind them as if they were going to throw them so I pulled my revolver out, had one leg over the side of the jeep as we were driving, with the gun pointed in the air in their direction. It was cocked and ready to go and as soon as they saw that they ran away. You never walked in front of a window, you crawled under it. It wasn't a very relaxing environment for any of us. You slept with your gun and it went with you everywhere you went. You never went into town alone and unarmed.

We were ordered to tour through one of the death camps, which was a horrible sight, with handcuffs on the wall, dark dingy cells, and a few of the ovens. It's dreadful how a man would treat another man, that's no way to treat a human being. I can't remember the name of the place, for obvious reasons, but General Eisenhower had ordered all troops in all services to see these camps so no one could say it was faked.

The Germans had breached the dams in Holland to flood the place. Armies were moving in waist deep water for the most part. At one point the Germans had arrived at a high dry place so our Army called us in from Antwerp to take care of them. At the time, we were part of an experiment using napalm, which is a nasty sticky burning material used mainly by flame throwers. They put two drop tanks on each of our airplanes, with Dick Sanwick, and I with Dick Austin and Scotty picked to fly over this German position. The napalm in the drop tanks were fused with hand grenade detonators--rather primitive but ... we took off, dive bombed over water, with no reference points to speak of except the high dry land. We dropped the bombs, returned to base and were never asked to use this napalm stuff again. While we were bombing them with this nasty stuff they were shooting at us, both coming in and going out so it wasn't a good situation for any of us. All four of us got back, with a few bullet holes here and there. I have no idea if the bombing run was or was not successful.

Prior to invading Germany, General Montgomery had laid 1,000 guns wheel to wheel and we were given the mission to go in ahead of the barrage just before the paratroopers were dropped on a suicidal mission that some idiot had decided on. This is where inefficiency enters into it. We were dive bombers and of course the Typhoon takes a lot of air to dive and pull out as you are carrying a lot of weight. Our mission was to cross the German border, to dive-bomb and isolate anti-aircraft positions going in at 1800 ft with anti-personnel bombs which are nasty little beasts and we carried two pods of them in at 1500 ft, lined up the target and by the time we let go, we were looking down the barrel of the anti-aircraft position. When we pulled out at about 200 ft, we were sitting ducks and at that height it was just like hitting us with a fly swatter. Three of us made it, but the fourth man didn't make it, which meant 25% of our strength were gone. We got the position and paid a dear price for it. We should have dive bombed from 8,000-10,000 ft to have enough speed to pull out.

BREMEN – GERMANY – 100 BOMBING MISSIONS

IN GERMANY, NEAR THE TOWN OF BREMEN, I WAS WANDERING around between flying and days off and I came across a brewery, where I walked through the door. It was full of huge vats of wine and mounds of sugar and potatoes. I was talking to the guard out front about Canada, home, food, the usual subjects. A little old lady came over to me with a shawl around her head; she couldn't speak English, but obviously came from the nearby women's labour camp. She rubbed her stomach, indicating hunger and needing food. I asked the young guard if he was guarding this building and he assured me he was. I asked him to walk a long tour along the edge of the perimeter and look out to the South . He said sure, he'd be glad to do that, what did I have in mind? I told him not to ask so he didn't need to worry about it. Off he went. I took the old lady into brewery and I pointed to the pile of potatoes and sugar so she went back to her camp, which was open, got all of her fellow detainees, and they brought bags, boxes, aprons and they cleaned that place out, you'd think it had been cleaned with a vacuum. When the guard came back he asked if everything was under control. I told him "absolutely". As his ranking officer he was required to do exactly what I told him to do; and as a very crabby ranking fighter pilot, I had no qualms about doing it. There was nothing anyone could do to me.

We had a German aircraft fly over our airstrip with a bed sheet hanging out of his cockpit.

He landed and I assume he became a prisoner of war. They marched him off and took his Messerschmitt 109 and parked it in the corner of the airfield. The war was winding down and that German pilot was all done and chose to surrender.

Our Wing and Squadron were moving into Germany but as of April 11, 1945 I had completed 84 operational trips in Europe and 26 operational trips in Alaska for the magic number of 100 which for a Fighter Pilot is called one tour so I was informed I had flown my final mission. The Wing Commander asked me to volunteer and test fly airplanes but I wanted none of it. I had pushed my luck as far as I could go; and if I was test flying sure as shooting something would blow up, so I declined. I then was scheduled to go to a rest camp for 30 days, which was as close to heaven as I could get at that time in my life. It was a tremendous relief, unbelievable relief to reach that 100, to know that you were done, if only temporarily. It was a tremendous morale booster as far as I was concerned.

War with Germany ceased at the end of April, 1945 so I was sent to England. While flying in a DC3 over Paris, the pilot informed us that the war was over in Europe. While in London, a keen British officer asked me to volunteer to do operations. My reply was not polite and I was slated for Burma.

We climbed on the Louis Pasteur in England to ship back to Canada. Because there were no submarines anymore, we shipped out with all lights blazing. They served white buns and butter, and it was an extravagance!. We shipped up to Montreal through the St. Lawrence Seaway, were put on a train to travel across Canada to Vancouver to board troop ships for Asia.

We were told we had one stop only, so rather than stop in Toronto to see all of my relatives; I went on to Calgary to stop and see my wife and baby. This highly annoyed the Toronto folks, of course, but they never did understand I had to follow orders. I phoned and explained it all to them, but it didn't get through to them.

We were sitting in the middle of Manitoba when the conductor came through and told us all about the Japanese surrender. I was slated for Burma and I would be flying a single-engine airplane with an air-cooled engine over the jungles. I was thrilled to not be visiting the jungles and snakes of Asia. That was the best news I ever had, and can accurately state that Harry Truman saved my life.

CANADA – SHIPPING TO PACIFIC – END OF WAR

MY WIFE ETHEL, MET ME IN THE CALGARY TRAIN STATION, RUN-ning down the train station, throwing herself into my arms.

We went over to the Palliser Hotel where I had a shower and tried to rejoin the human race. My next stop was to Colonel Belcher for my medical, a very casual once-over, which consisted of an aide hitting my back, which hurt, thanks to all of my airplane crashes. I got my discharge and I stood out in the street in Calgary with $100 from the government, a new suit which didn't fit, and a Canadian Maple Leaf pin. None of this could feed my family--no job, no house, no money.

On the trip back, I had run into my ex-padre who told me he had rounded up some jobs as trainees in a bakery company in Calgary at $30 per week. He asked me if I'd take it and I jumped at the opportunity. I had to report to an office at the Bakery in Calgary and the group there and introduced myself as a trainee in the management training program. They all laughed at me, and the son of the Bakery owner told someone to take this man to his horse. Jody, the barn man, was told to show me the horse and the manager left me to it. The barn master said here's your horse, his name is Pete. I patted this huge monster that turned his head, raised his lips and showed me his teeth. Jody said that meant he liked me and now I had to harness him, about which I knew nothing. He said all that leather strapping hung on the wall is to be thrown over the back of the horse. Jody showed me how to put it all together on the horse and then I had to put the bridle on including putting the bit in the horse's mouth.

I asked him how you make the horse go in reverse so I gave Pete a shove and he backed up. Fortunately Pete knew what he was to do and he got both of us to the wagon which I had to back Pete into and hitch up. I've gone from flying a 2,000 hp fighter plane, to driving a 1 hp horse.

I had no money left from my $100 and no clothes to go to work in, so I took the epaulettes off the battle dress I used to wear and it became my work dress. Door to door bread salesman, that was me.

Canada was not prepared to send troops to war nor was it prepared for their return. We did not get any assistance of any sort, not a GI Bill, not job training or a re-entry program, nothing.

I have lived a long, happy and productive life with my wonderful wife, Ethel, four children, grandchildren and great-grandchildren. I have undertaken telling my story of a time now long gone, which impacted me, as an individual in that great drama of World War II.

ACKNOWLEDGEMENTS

I WOULD LIKE TO EXPRESS MY GRATITUDE TO THE FOLLOWING people who have been most helpful to me in the production of this book.

First, I would like to thank my daughter, Linda Hilton for her work transcribing my memories, and my grandson, Geoffrey Kratz, for being our IT director and creating the means for the transcription to go back and forth between the U.S. and Canada. None of this would be possible without these great family members.

I would also like to thank Susanne Heaton, who worked on my behalf to secure the French and Dutch medals testifying to my service. In addition she arranged for my speech to the RCAF in Cold Lake, Alberta via her brother Colonel Alexander, Commander, RCAF Cold Lake.

Her efforts on my behalf cannot be understated.

The local newspaper, Airdrie Echo, have been very supportive

Acknowledgements

through their reporter, Chelsea Grainger who provided me with several interview opportunities, and provided editorial comments on the first daft. Loy Pacheco, staff at Cedarwood Station in Airdrie has provided invaluable assistance to a 96 year old man still learning Microsoft Word.

CPSIA information can be obtained
at www.ICGtesting.com
Printed in the USA
LVOW01s1543190116
471354LV00021B/1614/P